Out and About at the Vet Clinic

By Kitty Shea
Illustrated by Becky Shipe

Special thanks to our advisers for their expertise:

Cathy Sinning, D.V. M.
Minneapolis, Minnesota

Susan Kesselring, M.A., Literacy Educator
Rosemount-Apple Valley-Eagan (Minnesota) School District

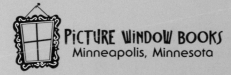

PICTURE WINDOW BOOKS
Minneapolis, Minnesota

The author wishes to thank:
Cathy Sinning, D.V. M., and Michelle Guertin, both of Alta Veterinary,
and Michelle Shriber, D.V. M., for their assistance with this book and their loving care of Alice.

Managing Editor: Bob Temple
Creative Director: Terri Foley
Editor: Peggy Henrikson
Editorial Adviser: Andrea Cascardi
Copy Editor: Laurie Kahn
Designer: John Moldstad
Page production: Picture Window Books
The illustrations in this book were prepared digitally.

Picture Window Books
5115 Excelsior Boulevard
Suite 232
Minneapolis, MN 55416
1-877-845-8392
www.picturewindowbooks.com

Library of Congress Cataloging-in-Publication Data
Shea, Kitty.
Out and about at the vet clinic / by Kitty Shea ; illustrated by Becky Shipe.
p. cm. — (Field trips)
Summary: Doctor Hart gives a guided tour of her veterinary clinic, where she explains
such things as what equipment she uses, how she calms animals down, and some of
the different problems she treats. Includes an activity and other learning resources.
Includes bibliographical references.
ISBN 1-4048-0296-7 (Reinforced Library Binding)
1. Veterinary hospitals—Juvenile literature. [1. Veterinary hospitals. 2. Veterinarians.]
I. Shipe, Becky, ill. II. Title. III. Field trips (Picture Window Books)
SF604.55 .S54 2004
636.08'32—dc22
                                    2003016159

We're going on a field trip to the vet clinic.
We can't wait!

Things to find out:

What kinds of animals do people bring to the vet?

Why don't some animals like going to the vet?

How do vets find out what's wrong with animals?

Do vets use the same tools to help animals that doctors use to help people?

Hi! Are you all here for checkups? Just kidding! Only animals have appointments at a veterinary clinic. I'm Dr. Hart, and I'm a veterinarian— a doctor for animals. People call me a vet for short. Our vet clinic sees mostly cats and dogs. People also bring in rabbits, ferrets, birds, reptiles, and rodents such as hamsters, rats, and gerbils.

Animals can't say where it hurts. Vets have to figure that out on their own. They learn how to do this by going to veterinary school for three or four years after college. Vets learn how to take care of many different kinds of animals.

5

Rocky, Ginger, and Cleo have appointments. It's good that Rocky and Ginger are on their leashes and Cleo is in her cat carrier. Otherwise, the dogs might chase Cleo.

	How the Vet Uses It
almoscope	to look into a pet's eyes
oscope	to look into a pet's ears
thermometer	to take a pet's temperature
stethoscope	to listen to a pet's heart
syringe	to give a shot or draw blood

Coming to the vet can scare and excite animals. Being scared or excited makes them shed fur. The clinic floor has to be swept several times a day to clean up all the hair.

Rocky is here for a checkup. Would you like to hear his heartbeat?
Thump-thump. Thump-thump. Thump-thump.

Now listen to your own heart. *Thump-thump. Thump-thump.*
A dog's heart beats faster than a person's.
It beats even faster if the dog is nervous.

Good dog, Rocky!

Vets use the same kind
stethoscopes that doctors
treat people use. Some vets
use adult-sized stethoscopes
for dogs and smaller, child-sized
stethoscopes for cats. It helps if
the owner is quiet when the ve
is listening to the pet's heart.

8

Vets use the same kind of stethoscopes that doctors who treat people use. Some vets use adult-sized stethoscopes for dogs and smaller, child-sized stethoscopes for cats. It helps if the owner is quiet when the vet is listening to the pet's heart.

Tool		How the Vet Uses It
	opthalmoscope	to look into a pet's eyes
	otoscope	to look into a pet's ears
	thermometer	to take a pet's temperature
	stethoscope	to listen to a pet's heart
	syringe	to give a shot or draw blood

Coming to the vet can scare and excite animals. Being scared or excited makes them shed fur. The clinic floor has to be swept several times a day to clean up all the hair.

Rocky is here for a checkup. Would you like to hear his heartbeat?
Thump-thump. Thump-thump. Thump-thump.

Now listen to your own heart. *Thump-thump. Thump-thump.*
A dog's heart beats faster than a person's.
It beats even faster if the dog is nervous.

Good dog, Rocky!

Look at all of these tools that help me examine Rocky!

Vets often keep treats in exam rooms to help their patients relax. Being at the vet is scary for some animals because they are in pain or afraid of people. Maybe they remember having an operation at the clinic. Using a soothing voice with pets can help calm them.

11

This is Mickie. She's our veterinary technician, or "vet tech" for short. Mickie helps me run tests and take X-rays. She's taking a picture of Ginger's leg, because Ginger has been limping lately. The X-ray will show if Ginger has any broken bones.

X-RAY

Vet techs wear special gowns, gloves, and neck shields. These help protect them from the rays of the X-ray machine. Too many rays over too many days can harm the technicians.

13

Cleo's chart shows she has lost weight since the last time she was here. Pete is holding Cleo while Mickie takes a blood sample to help find out why. We learn a lot about an animal's health from looking at things that may seem gross to you, such as blood and earwax. Vets are scientists, and scientists don't mind working with stuff like that!

Veterinary clinics run tests when animals are sick. Vets study samples under microscopes to see if everything looks normal. Clinics also own special testing machines. One of these machines can cost as much as a new car!

15

This is our operating room. Shhh. Let's not disturb our surgeon, Dr. Dean. He's taking a string out of Spinner's stomach. Spinner swallowed the string when he was playing with it and has been throwing up ever since.

Later, Dr. Dean will clean Daisy the dog's teeth. He gives both Spinner and Daisy shots to help them sleep right through their operations. That makes it easier for everyone!

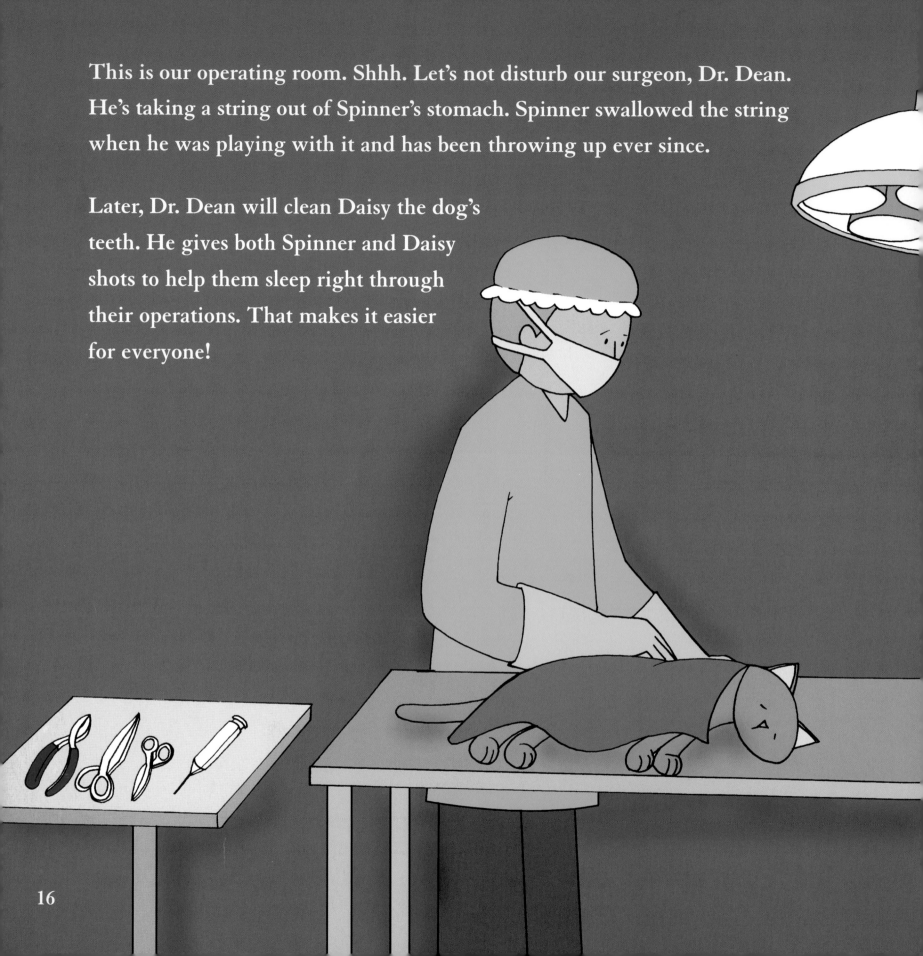

Spaying and neutering are among the most common surgeries at vet clinics. Animals can't have babies after these operations. This is good, because too many unwanted puppies and kittens end up at animal shelters.

Tell your pets "bowwow" and "meow" from me! Thanks for visiting the vet clinic. Bye!

HAPPY PETS
VETERINARY

ENTRANCE

GIVE YOUR PET A CHECKUP AT HOME

Note: If you do not have a pet, share this activity with a friend who has a pet. You can interview your friend about his or her pet and help your friend do the checkup.

What you need:
a marker
a self-stick label
a pocket folder
several sheets of paper
a pen or pencil
a pet

What you do:

1. Write the pet's name on the label with the marker, and stick the label on the front of the folder.
2. Write "Normal" at the top of one of the sheets of paper with the pen or pencil. This is where you will list what your pet is like normally. You need to know what's normal for your pet so you will know when something is wrong.
3. During the next few days, write down:
   • what and how much your pet eats;
   • how much water your pet drinks;
   • where your pet sleeps;
   • what your pet usually does during the day;
   • how your pet smells;
   • how your pet feels;
   • how your pet sounds.
4. Put the "Normal" list in one of the pockets of the folder. Put the blank sheets of paper in the other pocket.
5. Give your pet a checkup before its next appointment at the vet clinic. Or do a checkup if you think your pet is acting strangely. You might want to get in the habit of giving your pet a checkup every few months.
6. Write "Checkup" and the date at the top of one of the blank sheets of paper.
7. Read your "Normal" list. Then watch your pet for a few days. Look to see if anything is different from normal. For instance, is your pet scratching or sneezing more than usual? Is it limping? Do you feel any lumps on your pet's body? Does its breath smell different? Is it eating as much as it usually does? Write down your findings, then file your report in the folder.
8. If anything is different, tell an adult. The adult may decide to make an appointment for your pet at the vet clinic. If you wish, you may ask your vet for copies of any test results and add these to your folder at home. Ask the vet to explain what the results mean.

Remember, a healthy pet is a happy pet!

FUN FACTS

- More than 67,000 veterinarians work in the United States today. Nearly half of them work in clinics helping people's pets. Others teach in schools, do research in labs, or take care of animals at zoos or on farms. Some vets specialize in emergency care, surgery, or certain diseases.

- The first veterinary school was started in France in 1762. Before then, vets learned by working directly with animals.

- The letters D.V.M. after a vet's name stand for Doctor of Veterinary Medicine. Those letters mean the vet has successfully completed veterinary school and passed the test to get a veterinary license.

- The three most popular dog breeds in the United States are Labrador retrievers, golden retrievers, and German shepherds.

- Three out of 10 households in the United States own at least one cat. Four out of 10 households own at least one dog.

- Veterinary care is the most costly part of owning a pet. Cat owners spend an average of $104 on veterinary care each year. For dog owners, the average is $196. The next greatest expenses for a pet owner are food and then supplies, such as a collar, bowl, bed, or brush.

GLOSSARY

appointment—a plan to meet or see someone at a certain time

examine—to check an animal to gather information about its health

microscope—a tool that makes tiny things appear bigger

neuter—to do an operation on a male animal so he can't father babies

reptile—an egg-laying, cold-blooded animal with either no legs or short legs. A reptile usually has scales, like a snake, or a bony plate or plates, like a turtle. Lizards are also reptiles.

rodent—a warm-blooded animal that has large, sharp front teeth for gnawing things. Hamsters, mice, rats, and gerbils are rodents that people sometimes keep as pets.

spay—to do an operation on a female animal so she can't have babies

surgery—an operation that involves cutting into the body to remove or fix a part of the body

veterinary technician (vet tech)—a veterinarian's helper. A vet tech usually does lab work and takes X-rays.

X-ray—a picture taken of the inside of the body that can show if something is wrong

TO LEARN MORE

At the Library

Flanagan, Alice K. *Dr. Friedman Helps Animals.* New York: Children's Press, 1999.

Gibbons, Gail. *Say Woof! The Day of a Country Veterinarian.* New York: Maxwell Macmillan International, 1992.

Leonard, Marcia. *The Pet Vet.* Brookfield, Conn.: Millbrook Press, 1999.

Raatma, Lucia. *Veterinarians.* Minneapolis: Compass Point Books, 2003.

Walker-Hodge, Judith. *Animal Hospital.* New York: DK Pub., 1999.

On the Web

Fact Hound offers a safe, fun way to find Web sites related to this book. All of the sites on Fact Hound have been researched by our staff. *http://www.facthound.com*

1. Visit the Fact Hound home page.
2. Enter a search word related to this book, or type in this special code: 1404802967.
3. Click on the FETCH IT button.

Your trusty Fact Hound will fetch the best sites for you!

INDEX